SCHOLASTIC

FIERCE AND FEROCIOUS

Bees do more than buzz

by Lucy Waterhouse

make
believe
ideas

At the park, Tom jumped behind his sister.
"Why are you hiding?" asked Kate.
"The bees! They might sting me," said Tom.

"They'll only sting you if you hurt them," Kate said. "Bees are our friends. Let me show you how useful they are."

These bees are carrying pollen from one flower to another.

I can see the pollen on this bee's legs.

Plants need pollen to make seeds.
The seeds grow into new plants.
Without bees, some plants could die out.

Much of our food comes from plants. Without bees, we would have less to eat.

This beekeeper thinks bees are useful, too. She collects some of the honey that the bees make.

Without bees, we would have no honey.

11

I wonder if other people know how much bees help us? I'm going to tell everyone how useful they are.

How Bees Help Us

Bees help plants make seeds.

Discussion Questions

1. Where is the pollen on the bee's body?

2. How do we get honey?

3. Do you think bees are important? Why?

SIGHT WORDS

Learning sight words helps you read fluently.
Practice these sight words from the book.
Use them in sentences of your own.

eat see how much from think these would could